# KNOWING GOD FOR YOURSELF

## A Devotional to Deepen Your Relationship with God

*By*

*Ester Jamera*

This devotional or parts thereof may not be reproduced without prior written permission of the author except as provided by the International Copyright Law.

Unless otherwise stated, all scripture in this devotional is taken from the New International Version (NIV) of the Bible ©Zondervan Corporation. Scripture quotation marked NKJV is from the New King James Version sourced from YouVersion.com.

© Ester Jamera 2024

# Table of Contents

Dedication .................................................................................................................. i
Acknowledgement ..................................................................................................... ii
Knowing God for Yourself – Why It Matters............................................................. 1
Knowing God for Yourself in Scripture .................................................................... 3
Overview of the 31 Days ........................................................................................... 5
Day 1: The Trinity ...................................................................................................... 6
Day 2: God's Character ............................................................................................. 8
Day 3: God's Attributes ........................................................................................... 10
Day 4: God's Names ................................................................................................ 13
Day 5: Faith and Trust ............................................................................................. 15
Day 6: Intimacy with God ........................................................................................ 17
Day 7: Identity in Christ........................................................................................... 19
Day 8: Nurturing Spiritual Disciplines and Practices ............................................ 21
Day 9: Discerning God's Voice ............................................................................... 23
Day 10: The Holy Spirit ........................................................................................... 25
Day 11: Obedience and Sacrifice ........................................................................... 27
Day 12: Audacious Faith ......................................................................................... 29
Day 13: Cultivating Audacious Faith ...................................................................... 32
Day 14: The Power of Our Words ........................................................................... 34
Day 15: Ambassadors of Christ .............................................................................. 36
Day 16: The Call to Evangelism .............................................................................. 38
Day 17: Overcoming Barriers to Intimacy with God .............................................. 40
Day 18: The Transformative Power of Repentance ............................................... 42
Day 19: Burden of the Word ................................................................................... 44
Day 20: Prayerful Reflection ................................................................................... 46
Day 21: Pursuing Spiritual Growth ......................................................................... 48
Day 22: Carrying Your Cross Daily (Part 1) ............................................................ 50
Day 23: Carrying Your Cross Daily (Part 2) ............................................................ 52
Day 24: Embracing God's Grace ............................................................................ 54
Day 25. Discovering Your Purpose ........................................................................ 56
Day 26: Functioning in Your Purpose .................................................................... 58

Day 27: Finding Beauty in Discouragement .................................................................. 60
Day 28: Knowing and Overcoming the Enemy ........................................................... 62
Day 29: Strength in Godly Friendships ......................................................................... 64
Day 30: Serving the Lord with Heart, Body and Soul ................................................. 66
Day 31: Thriving in Your Faith Sustainably ................................................................. 68

# Dedication

Dear God

Thank you for loving me.

# Acknowledgement

To Vanessa Riley, Marisol Pena, Rachel Aston, and Travis Graham thank you for combing through the manuscript and sharing your insights. God bless you today and always!

# Knowing God for Yourself – Why It Matters

Knowing God for ourselves holds significant importance for various reasons. It is essential for establishing a personal relationship with Him, strengthening our faith, nurturing spiritual growth, seeking His guidance, and finding solace and strength in His presence. It is a practice that requires intentional pursuit and a genuine desire to know Him more intimately. This intentional pursuit leads to profound benefits in our lives, from our identity and purpose to our relationship with others, the decisions we make, and our general outlook on life. Let's explore some of these specific benefits:

- **Intimacy and Fellowship**: Just as in any relationship, knowing someone personally involves spending time with them, communicating, and understanding their character and desires. Similarly, knowing God for ourselves involves building a personal relationship with Him through prayer, studying His Word, and experiencing His presence in our lives. This intimacy fosters a deeper connection with Him, leading to a richer and more fulfilling spiritual life.

- **Spiritual Growth**: Knowing God for ourselves is essential for our spiritual growth. As we spend time seeking and knowing Him, we learn more about His character, His Will for our lives, and how He desires us to live. This knowledge transforms us and helps us grow spiritually.

- **Discernment:** Knowing God for ourselves enables us to discern His voice and follow His guidance in our lives. When we have a personal relationship with God, we can seek His wisdom to distinguish between truth and falsehood, and direction in making decisions, responding to challenges, and navigating life in general.

- **Strength and Comfort**: In times of difficulty, knowing God for ourselves provides strength, comfort, and hope. We can draw on our personal experiences of His faithfulness, love, and grace to sustain us through trials and tribulations.

- **Identity, Purpose and Eternal Perspective**: Knowing God for ourselves helps us understand our identity and purpose in Him. As we grow in our knowledge of who God is and how He sees us, we discover our true identity as His beloved children and understand the unique purpose He has for us. This understanding also gives us an eternal perspective on life. It helps us focus on what truly matters, enabling us to live with a sense of purpose and hope that transcends temporal circumstances.

- **Witness and Evangelism**: Knowing God for ourselves empowers us to be effective witnesses for Him. When we have personally experienced His love, grace, and power in our lives, we are better equipped and empowered to share our faith with others and lead them into a personal relationship with God.

- **Authentic Faith:** When we know God for ourselves, our faith becomes more authentic and genuine. We don't rely solely on what others say about God or their experiences with Him; instead, we have our own firsthand encounters and experiences that deepen our faith.

# Knowing God for Yourself in Scripture

- This is what the Lord says: 'Let not the wise boast of their wisdom or the strong boast of their strength or the rich boast of their riches but let the one who boasts boast about this: that they have the understanding to know me, that I am the Lord, who exercises kindness, justice and righteousness on earth, for in these I delight,' declares the LORD. - **Jeremiah 9:23-24**

- But seek first his kingdom and his righteousness, and all these things will be given to you as well. - **Matthew 6:33**

- The people who know their God shall be strong and carry out *great exploits.* - **Daniel 11:32b NKJV**

- My heart says of you, 'Seek his face!' Your face, LORD, I will seek. - **Psalms 27:8**

- You, God, are my God, earnestly I seek you; I thirst for you, my whole being longs for you, in a dry and parched land where there is no water. - **Psalms 63:1**

- My ears had heard of you, but now my eyes have seen you. - **Job 42:5**

- I sought the LORD, and he answered me; he delivered me from all my fears. Those who looked to him are radiant; their faces are never covered with shame. - **Psalms 34:4-5**

- They said to the woman, 'We no longer believe just because of what you said; now we have heard for ourselves, and we know that this man really is the Savior of the world.' - **John 4:42**

- Those who know your name trust in you, for you, LORD, have never forsaken those who seek you. - **Psalms 9:10**

- What is more, I consider everything a loss because of the surpassing worth of knowing Christ Jesus my Lord, for whose sake I have lost all things. I consider them garbage, that I may gain Christ and be found in him, not having a righteousness of my own that comes from the law, but that which is through faith in Christ—the righteousness that comes from God on the basis of faith. I want to know Christ— yes, to know the power of his resurrection... - **Philippians 3:8-10a**

Welcome to **'Knowing God for Yourself,'** a 31-day devotional designed to deepen your relationship with God and ignite a fresh passion for spiritual growth. Nowadays, life seems to move at an ever-increasing pace, leaving us caught up in a whirlwind of responsibilities and distractions. In this constant busyness, it is all too easy to lose sight of what truly matters – our connection with our Creator. This devotional aims to guide you through introspective reflections and thought-provoking questions to assess and enhance your spiritual journey.

Each day of this devotional has been thoughtfully put together to examine different facets of your understanding of and relationship with God. From exploring the Trinity and God's character to nurturing spiritual disciplines and embracing your purpose, we will consider topics such as faith, intimacy with God, obedience, and the transformative power of repentance.

Scripture references are provided for each day to support you in your exploration, allowing the Holy Spirit to guide you as you reflect on the questions and insights presented. You will find a full list of the Scriptures in a table provided at the end of this devotional. The Scripture references serve as a starting point, so you are highly encouraged to consider other Scriptures and resources to gain a comprehensive understanding of the themes being explored. This approach fosters a unique and intimate encounter with God, tailored to your individual experiences and aspirations.

Throughout this process, you will confront challenges, experience moments of revelation, and cultivate a deeper insight into who God is to you and who you are in Him. By engaging with the reflections and questions given as a minimum, you'll not only assess your current spiritual state but also uncover areas for growth and transformation. May your heart be open, your Spirit receptive, and your mind prepared to encounter the living God in a new and profound way.

All the best with your exploration.

Much Love

Ester

# Overview of the 31 Days

| Day 1: The Trinity | Day 2: God's Character | Day 3: God's Attributes | Day 4: God's Names | Day 5: Faith and Trust |
|---|---|---|---|---|
| Day 6: Intimacy with God | Day 7: Identity In Christ | Day 8: Nurturing Spiritual Disciplines | Day 9: Discerning God's Voice | Day 10: The Holy Spirit |
| Day 11: Obedience | Day 12: Audacious Faith | Day 13: Cultivating Audacious Faith | Day 14: The Power of Our Words | Day 15: Ambassadors of Christ |
| Day 16: The Call to Evangelism | Day 17: Overcoming Barriers to Intimacy with God | Day 18: The Transformative Power of Repentance | Day 19: Burden of the Word | Day 20: Prayerful Reflection |
| Day 21: Pursuing Spiritual Growth | Day 22: Carrying Your Cross Daily Part 1 | Day 23: Carrying Your Cross Daily Part 2 | Day 24: Embracing God's Grace | Day 25: Discovering Your Purpose |
| Day 26: Functioning in Your Purpose | Day 27: Finding Beauty in Discouragement | Day 28: Knowing and Overcoming the Enemy | Day 29: Strength in Godly Friendships | Day 30: Serving the Lord with Heart, Body and Soul |
| Day 31: Thriving in Your Faith Sustainably | | | | |

# Day 1: The Trinity

Welcome to Day 1 of our devotional journey! Let's start by exploring the nature of God – God the Father, Son, and Holy Spirit. As we contemplate the Trinity, we're invited to ponder on the very essence of God Himself – three persons in perfect unity and relationship. It is a concept that stretches our finite minds, yet it lies at the core of our Christian faith and shapes our understanding of God's nature and character.

Today's reflection prompts us to consider how we would introduce God to someone who knows nothing about Him and reflect on the profound impact of Jesus and the role of the Holy Spirit in our lives. As we engage with the reflection questions, may we be open to the mystery and wonder of the Trinity, allowing it to deepen our reverence for God and his sovereignty.

**Reference Scriptures**

- Matthew 28:19
- 2 Corinthians 13:14
- John 14:26

**Reflection Questions**

- If you were to introduce God to someone who knows nothing about Him, what would you say?
- Can you articulate your beliefs about Jesus Christ and His significance in your faith?
- How would you describe the Holy Spirit's role in your life and the life of the Church?

# NOTES

# Day 2: God's Character

In the Bible, we encounter various facets of God's character – from His unconditional love, grace, and mercy to His justice, jealousy, and righteous wrath against sin. It is important to recognise that God's character is multifaceted and encompasses both His compassion and His holiness. His love and grace extend to all, offering forgiveness and redemption to those who seek Him. His righteousness and justice highlight the consequences of sin and disobedience.

God's righteous wrath, jealousy, and justice are often mentioned in response to human actions such as idolatry and persistent disobedience. In the Old Testament, idolatry involved worshipping and revering man-made gods or deities. Today, idolatry often arises from misplaced desires and priorities, shifting our focus away from God and compromising His central place in our lives.

As we explore God's character, let us embrace His love and grace while also acknowledging His expectations of us. May we endeavour to align our desires and priorities with His Will, seeking to honour Him in all aspects of our lives.

**Reference Scriptures**

- Exodus 34:6-7
- Lamentations 3:22-23
- Romans 8:28

**Reflection Questions**

- How have you experienced the multifaceted nature of God's character in your life?

    Reflect on moments where you've encountered His love and mercy, as well as instances where you've seen His justice and righteousness at work, whether directly or indirectly.

- Given all your daily responsibilities, how do you prioritise spending time with God and what aspects of your faith help you navigate uncertainty and adversity in life?

- In what ways do you actively seek to understand and reflect the qualities of God's character in your interactions with others?

# NOTES

# Day 3: God's Attributes

Today, we will be digging deeper into the awe-inspiring attributes of our Creator. As we embark on this exploration, we are reminded of the profound truth that we serve an ever-watchful God whose love and care for us surpass our understanding. Despite the challenges and uncertainties we may face, His presence is constant, His power unwavering, and His knowledge boundless.

At the heart of God's character lie His key attributes: omnipotent, omniscient, and omnipresent. These attributes serve as pillars of His sovereignty and majesty, revealing the depth of His love and the extent of His involvement in our lives.

**Omnipotent:** This attribute speaks to the all-encompassing power of God. He is not limited by any external forces or constraints; rather, He holds absolute authority and control over every aspect of creation. In times of weakness or struggle, we can find strength and assurance in knowing that our God is mighty to save and is ever ready to fight our battles.

**Omniscient:** God's omniscience reflects His perfect knowledge and understanding of all things. There is nothing hidden from His sight and no detail too small for His attention. He sees beyond our outward appearance and understands the deepest desires of our hearts. He knows our past, present and future. In moments of doubt or confusion, we can take comfort in the knowledge that God sees us, knows us, and cares for us intimately.

**Omnipresent:** Perhaps most comforting of all is the assurance that God is always with us. His omnipresence means that God is present everywhere at all times; there is no place where he is not; whether we find ourselves in moments of joy or sorrow, in times of abundance or scarcity, God is there, walking alongside us and offering His unfailing love and support. We are God Protected around the clock!

**Reference Scriptures**

- Psalm 139:7-10
- Isaiah 40:28
- Hebrews 4:13

**Reflection Questions**

- On a scale of 0 - 10 (0 being no belief, 10 being complete belief), how much do you personally embrace the omnipotent, omniscient, and omnipresent nature of God? What is the reason for your score?
- In what practical ways do you integrate the understanding of God's attributes into

your daily decision-making process?
- How does your understanding of God's omnipotence influence your response to challenges and difficulties in your life?

# NOTES

# Day 4: God's Names

Our God is a trinitarian God with three persons, God the Father, God the Son and God the Holy Spirit. But He is also known by various names and titles throughout the Old and New Testaments.

Today, let's journey into the depths of God's names – there are over a hundred to explore! These names, rather than referring to the different persons of God, serve as windows to the multifaceted nature of His character. From Elohim, signifying His might and power, to Adonai, denoting His lordship and mastery, some of the most common names of God include Jehovah Jireh, the Lord who provides; Jehovah Rapha, the Lord who heals; and El Shaddai, God Almighty. Each name carries a unique revelation of God's character and His promises to His people, revealing more fully who He is and how He desires his people to relate to Him. This fosters a deeper and richer intimacy with Him.

May this journey of introspection deepen your connection with the Almighty and reveal new dimensions of His character, empowering you to walk in greater faith and confidence.

**Reference Scriptures**

- Exodus 3:14
- Isaiah 9:6
- Philippians 2:9-11

**Reflection Questions**

- Which name or title of God resonates with you the most, and why?
- Do you find yourself drawn more to names that highlight God's power and might, or those emphasising His compassion and love? Reflect on why you feel drawn to certain attributes of God's character and how this influences your perception of Him.
- If you were to choose a name or title to address God in your prayers, which one would it be, and what significance does it hold for you?

# NOTES

# Day 5: Faith and Trust

Today, let's focus on the bedrock of our relationship with God: Faith and Trust. In a world marked by uncertainties and the ups and downs of life, our faith and trust in God become the anchors that steady our souls in the storm.

Faith means having a feeling of certainty in someone or something, especially without tangible evidence. In our context, it is the assurance of things hoped for, the conviction of things not seen, and complete confidence in God's intentions and ability to come through for us. Faith serves as the foundation of our relationship with him and his promises to and for us.

Trust is reliance and dependence on something or someone's ability, strength, or truth. In our Christian walk, this means believing in God's reliability and acknowledging His sovereignty - accepting as true what He says about Himself, His Word, His abilities, and His strength. This involves placing our confidence in His faithfulness to fulfill His promises, to continue loving us and to work tirelessly for our good.

**Reference Scriptures**

- Hebrews 11:1
- Proverbs 3:5-6
- Mark 11:22-24

**Reflection Questions**

- How would you describe your faith in God at this moment in your life? Are there specific areas of your life (e.g. career, relationships, family, finances, church life, friendships) where you exercise more or less faith? Why?
- Are there specific aspects of God's character or promises that you find most challenging to trust in?
- Reflect on a time when your faith was tested, and you had to lean on God's promises. How did this experience shape your trust in Him?

# NOTES

# Day 6: Intimacy with God

Today, our focus is on exploring the concept of intimacy with God. Intimacy involves a close, personal relationship marked by a deep connection, familiarity, vulnerability, and transparency. As believers, cultivating intimacy with God goes beyond mere knowledge; it is about experiencing His presence, understanding His heart, and developing a genuine hunger and thirst for more of Him. It is in this intimate space of communion with God that we discover the richness of His love, the wisdom of His guidance, and the comfort of His companionship.

**Reference Scriptures**

- Jeremiah 29:13
- Psalm 27:8
- John 15:5

**Reflection Questions**

- What do you understand by the term intimacy? How do you cultivate your intimacy with God?
- On a scale of 0 - 10 (0 being no sense of connectedness, 10 being the highest level of connectedness imaginable), how would you gauge your present connectedness to God? Why?
- How do you typically respond to being challenged and stretched in your faith journey?

# NOTES

# Day 7: Identity in Christ

Identity refers to the collection of characteristics that uniquely distinguish and define a person or a thing. We can conclude that our new identity in Christ should be recognisable both to ourselves and to others. When we embrace our identity in Christ, we can live with confidence, knowing that we are deeply loved, forgiven, and accepted.

More importantly, how we perceive ourselves directly influences the depth of our intimacy with God. When we align our identity with His truth, our connection with Him becomes more authentic and transformative.

**Reference Scriptures**

- 2 Corinthians 5:17
- 1 Peter 2:9
- Romans 8:17

**Reflection Questions**

- How would you describe your current perception of yourself? What factors influence this perception?
- What biblical truths or promises have shaped your identity in Christ? How often do you meditate on these truths?
- On a scale of 0 - 10 (0 being uncertain, 10 being very confident), how confident are you in your identity in Christ?

**Bonus Question:** How do you safeguard yourself from external opinions or societal standards defining your identity?

# NOTES

# Day 8: Nurturing Spiritual Disciplines and Practices

In our walk of faith, engaging in spiritual disciplines and practices is not only beneficial but also essential for our growth, maturity, and deepening relationship with God. Among other things, these spiritual disciplines and practices encompass various aspects such as prayer, fellowship, solitude, reading the Bible, and sharing our testimonies.

Prayer serves as a vital means of communication with our Heavenly Father, enabling us to express gratitude, seek guidance, and experience His presence. Fellowship with other believers provides opportunities for mutual encouragement, accountability, and spiritual growth within the community. Solitude offers precious moments of quiet reflection and intimacy with God, allowing us to hear His voice and receive His comfort and guidance. Reading the Bible nourishes our souls and shapes our understanding of God's character, His promises, and His Will for our lives. Sharing our testimonies allows us to bear witness to God's faithfulness and work in our lives, inspiring and encouraging others in their faith journeys.

In reflecting on these various spiritual disciplines and practices, I invite you to set aside some time for introspection and evaluation of your engagement with each one. As you do so, seek to deepen your connection with God and allow these practices to enrich your faith.

**Reference Scriptures**

- 1 Timothy 4:7-8
- Psalm 119:11
- Colossians 3:16

**Reflection Questions**

- Reflect on your daily spiritual practices. What routines or habits contribute to your spiritual well-being? Are there areas where you'd like to intentionally grow?
- How do you proactively prevent the demands of daily life and complacency from hindering your effective engagement in spiritual practices?
- How does your engagement in spiritual practices contribute to the spiritual well-being of those around you?

# NOTES

# Day 9: Discerning God's Voice

Our minds are often filled with a myriad of thoughts; decisions to make, and considerations to contend with. Discerning God's voice and distinguishing it from our own desires or the schemes of the enemy is a daily challenge for many of us. In this daily struggle, we are called to seek clarity and guidance from the Lord.

Discerning God's voice requires a deliberate and attentive posture of the heart, characterised by humility, prayerfulness, and a deep reliance on His Word. It involves a process of filtering through the various voices and influences that vie for our attention and aligning our thoughts and decisions with the truths revealed in Scripture. We can achieve this by seeking his wisdom, testing the spirits, and submitting our desires to God's Will.

Let's pause and reflect on the methods and criteria we employ in discerning God's voice. May we cultivate a sensitivity to His leading, allowing His voice to permeate through the noise and guide our steps along the path of righteousness.

**Reference Scriptures**

- John 10:27
- 1 Kings 19:11-12
- Isaiah 30:21

**Reflection Questions**

- How do you distinguish God's voice from your own thoughts and desires or external influences?
- What clues or confirmation did you receive to affirm you are hearing from God?
- How do you manage situations where external pressures or societal norms clash with what you believe God is prompting you to do?

# NOTES

# Day 10: The Holy Spirit

In our ongoing exploration of knowing God on a deeper and more intimate level, today, we turn our attention to the Holy Spirit – a divine gift from God. The Holy Spirit, often referred to as the third person of the Trinity, has many roles and functions serving as our guide, comforter, and a source of divine wisdom. As our comforter, He offers solace in times of distress, wrapping us in His tender embrace and filling us with peace that surpasses all understanding. As a source of divine wisdom, the Holy Spirit imparts insight, equipping us to navigate life's complexities with clarity and purpose.

Let's take a moment to reflect on the profound significance of the Holy Spirit in our lives. How do we perceive His presence and activity in our daily experiences? How do we actively engage with Him in our spiritual practices and decision-making processes? As we invest in understanding the role of the Holy Spirit, may we open our hearts to His leading and surrender to His transformative power in our lives.

**Reference Scriptures**

- Acts 1:8
- John 14:26
- Romans 8:26

**Reflection Questions**

- How would you describe your current understanding of the Holy Spirit's role in your life?
- In what ways do you actively seek the guidance of the Holy Spirit in your decision-making and daily activities?
- How do you cultivate an ongoing relationship with the Holy Spirit, allowing Him to shape your character and guide your walk with God?

# NOTES

# Day 11: Obedience and Sacrifice

Obedience and sacrifice are fundamental and interconnected aspects of our relationship with God, reflecting our deep commitment to His Will and purpose for our lives. While practices like prayer and fasting are essential, they don't replace the crucial role obedience and sacrifice play in the manifestation of what we are hoping for and the strength of our relationship with God.

Obedience, as emphasised in Scripture, is about aligning our hearts and actions with God's Will. It is the intentional choice to follow His guidance and instructions, demonstrating our trust in His sovereignty and our commitment to His purposes for our lives. Sacrifice, on the other hand, often requires giving up something valuable or meaningful in obedience or devotion to God. It may involve sacrificing time, resources, comforts, or desires to honour God and fulfill His plan.

As we reflect on the significance of obedience and sacrifice in our faith journey, let's examine our hearts and commit ourselves to a life marked by voluntary submission to God's Will. Through obedience and sacrifice, we position ourselves to experience the fullness of God's Will and purpose for our lives.

**Reference Scriptures**

- 1 John 2:3-6
- James 1:22
- Romans 6:16

**Reflection Questions**

- On a scale of 0 to 10 (0 Not obedient at all and 10 Complete Obedience), how do you rate your obedience to the promptings of the Holy Spirit and God's Word? Are there areas of your life where you find obedience to be more challenging? If so, what steps can you take to foster greater obedience in those areas?
- How do you balance the tension between taking intentional steps of obedience and relying on God's grace in your faith journey?
- Reflect on a time when your obedience led to a noticeable blessing or breakthrough in your life. What lessons did you learn from that experience?

# NOTES

# Day 12: Audacious Faith

As followers of Christ and children of God, empowered by the Holy Spirit, we are called to exercise audacious faith, a faith that believes in the extraordinary power of God working within us. Throughout the Bible, we see examples of individuals who demonstrated such faith and accomplished remarkable feats. Consider characters like David, who faced Goliath with unyielding trust in God's strength, or Daniel, who stood firm in his faith in the lion's den. Abraham, Moses, Joseph, Joshua, Enoch, Shammah, Eleazar, Philip, Paul, Naomi, Ruth, Esther, and countless others exemplify this audacious faith.

As we marvel at the incredible acts of faith by these heroes of our faith, it is important to remember that they, too, faced moments of doubt and uncertainty. They wrestled with their faith, questioned their abilities, and grappled with fears just like we do. Yet, in their weakness, they found strength in God's promises. Their stories remind us that God is patient with our doubts and struggles, waiting with a welcoming embrace to strengthen and guide us. So, take heart, knowing that the same God who worked wonders through them is at work within you, ready to turn your struggles into triumphs for His glory.

The question we must confront today is whether we truly believe that the same power that worked in these heroes of faith also resides within us. Do we have the audacity to trust God for what may seem impossible from a worldly perspective? It is a challenge for us to step back and evaluate the depth of our faith – a faith that dares to believe in God's boundless power and promises, even when circumstances appear hopeless.

Let's take a moment to reflect on the depth of our faith. How do we respond to life's challenges? Remember, the Bible showcases incredible examples of faithful individuals who experienced moments of hesitation alongside bold acts of faith. Each of us is unique, but we serve the same God who is willing and able to turn any situation around for our good and his glory!

**Reference Scriptures**

- Matthew 17:20
- Hebrews 11:1
- Mark 9:23

**Reflection Questions**

- What is the most daring thing you've done in faith, and what was the result?
- Are there specific biblical stories of audacious faith that inspire and guide your own faith journey?

- How does your knowledge and understanding of God's character influence your confidence in taking bold steps of faith?

**Bonus Question:** The Bible states that we are made in God's image. What does this mean to you?

# NOTES

# Day 13: Cultivating Audacious Faith

As we continue our journey of knowing God for ourselves, let's take a moment to look at how we can cultivate audacious faith. Audacious faith goes beyond the ordinary. It dares to believe in God's extraordinary power and promises. It is a faith that takes bold steps, trusting in God, who can do immeasurably more than we can ask or imagine. It is rooted in a deep trust in the character of God and His ability to accomplish the impossible through us.

Cultivating audacious faith requires intentional effort and a deliberate mindset shift. It involves stepping out of our comfort zones and embracing a posture of boldness and confidence in God's sovereignty. It means choosing to trust in God's promises, even when circumstances seem bleak, and holding fast to His Word as the ultimate source of truth and guidance.

Using the given reflection questions, let's explore how we can cultivate audacious faith in our daily lives. May this exploration lead to a deeper understanding of what audacious faith looks like and inspire us to live boldly for the glory of God.

**Reference Scriptures**

- Romans 10:17
- Hebrews 11:6
- James 1:6

**Reflection Questions**

- In your own words, how would you define audacious faith? What does it look like to you?
- How does fear or doubt hinder your ability to embrace audacious faith? What strategies can you employ to overcome fear and doubt?
- In what areas of your life do you feel God may be calling you to step out in audacious faith? What has been your response so far, and how do you feel about it?

# NOTES

# Day 14: The Power of Our Words

Understanding the profound impact of our words is crucial in developing and sustaining God-kind of faith (audacious faith). Just as God spoke creation into existence, our words possess the power to shape our spiritual landscape and influence the quality of our lives. The Bible affirms this truth in Proverbs where it declares that death and life are in the power of the tongue. The words we speak to ourselves and others carry weight and significance. They have the potential to either build up or tear down, inspire faith, or instill doubt and bring life or death. They mould our perceptions, shape our attitudes, and ultimately have an impact on our relationship with God and others.

When we align our words with God's truth and promises, we create an environment conducive to nurturing audacious faith. Conversely, negative and faithless words can hinder our spiritual growth and impede our ability to trust in God's power and promises.

May the following reflection questions inspire you to always speak life-giving words that promote a vibrant and thriving faith in God.

**Reference Scriptures**

- Proverbs 18:21
- Ephesians 4:29
- Matthew 12:36

**Reflection Questions**

- How does the concept of speaking things into existence align with your understanding of faith?
- How much do you think your words have played a role in shaping your faith and daily life so far?
- In what ways do you intentionally feed your Spirit with positive and faith-filled words?

# NOTES

# Day 15: Ambassadors of Christ

An ambassador is a respected official acting as a representative of a nation. Sent to a foreign land, the ambassador's role is to reflect the official position of the sovereign body that gave him authority. As Christians, we are ambassadors of Christ, entrusted with the gospel; and our role is to reflect the 'official position' of heaven in this world. Wow! How amazing is that?

What we are seeing here is that knowing God for ourselves involves the understanding that we are representing him in the world. He requires us to work. The Bible talks about the harvest being plentiful, but the workers few. Let's take some time to reflect on what it means to be an ambassador of Christ and how you can carry the message of salvation to those within your sphere of influence.

**Reference Scriptures**

- 2 Corinthians 5:20
- Ephesians 6:19-20
- Philippians 2:13

**Reflection Questions**

- What does being an ambassador of Christ mean to you personally?
- How are you actively fulfilling your role as an ambassador of Christ and contributing to the work of the Kingdom?
- In what ways does your identity as an ambassador of Christ influence your interactions with others within the church community and beyond?

# NOTES

# Day 16: The Call to Evangelism

Expanding on the theme of being ambassadors of Christ and recognising the abundant harvest with few workers, we are reminded of the Great Commission in Matthew 28:19-20 where Jesus commands us to "Go and make disciples of all nations..." As ambassadors, we carry the responsibility of sharing the gospel message with others, and actively engaging in the work of evangelism. This entails not only proclaiming the Good News but also living lives that reflect the transformative power of the Gospel.

Today, let's reflect on our personal experiences with evangelism, exploring any barriers we may encounter and seeking ways to overcome them. May our reflections lead us to a deeper understanding of our role in spreading the message of our faith and inspire us to engage more intentionally in fulfilling the call to evangelism in our lives and communities.

**Reference Scriptures**

- Matthew 28:19-20
- Acts 1:8
- Romans 10:14

**Reflection Questions**

- Reflecting on the urgency of the plentiful harvest with few workers, how does this awareness impact your sense of responsibility in sharing the gospel?
- What has been your experience in sharing the gospel with others?
- Are there any fears or barriers you've encountered in evangelism? How can you overcome or address these challenges?

# NOTES

# Day 17: Overcoming Barriers to Intimacy with God

As we continue our journey of knowing God for ourselves, it is essential to recognise and address barriers that might hinder our intimacy with Him. These barriers, such as disobedience, can create distance between us and our Creator, preventing the deep connection we desire.

Building on our exploration of obedience and sacrifice on Day 11, let's turn our attention to addressing specific barriers that might impede our connection with God. These barriers include thoughts, words, desires, actions, or inactions that are contrary to God's precepts, or fall short of them.

So you can see, the barriers to intimacy with God can be complex and wide-ranging, making it worthwhile to explore these in Scripture to ensure that our understanding of and response to these barriers is grounded in God's Word.

Through practices such as prayer, study of Scripture, and dependence on the Holy Spirit, we can be equipped and empowered to overcome barriers to our relationship with God and pave the way for a deeper, more intimate relationship with our Heavenly Father. This involves acknowledging the presence of sin in our lives, if there is any and seeking repentance and forgiveness through Christ.

**Reference Scriptures**

- Psalm 139:23-24
- Proverbs 18:24
- Hebrews 4:16

**Reflection Questions**

- To what extent are you intentional in creating space and time to explore any areas of your life that may be creating distance between you and God?
- What, if any, are some specific barriers that you feel may be currently affecting your intimacy with God?
- How do you approach confession and repentance in your spiritual life? Are there steps you can take to make this process more intentional and sincere?

# NOTES

# Day 18: The Transformative Power of Repentance

Building on the theme of sin and overcoming barriers to intimacy with God, let's turn our focus on repentance. In Scripture, repentance is portrayed as a fundamental shift from rejection or indifference towards Christ to embracing faith in Him. Repentance is widely understood as an acknowledgment of our shortcomings, a turning away from them, and a deliberate effort to live a life that pleases God and reflects His character. Genuine faith in Jesus inevitably leads to a transformation of behaviour, as repentance involves a holistic change of heart and mind.

As we reflect on the transformative power of repentance, let's consider how our changed behaviours and attitudes have contributed to a more intimate relationship with God. Through introspection and prayer, check whether there are areas where repentance may be needed and allow yourself to experience the liberating grace and forgiveness that come from turning towards God in true repentance.

**Reference Scriptures**

- Acts 3:19
- Ezekiel 18:30
- 1 John 1:9

**Reflection Questions**

- How would you define repentance? What does it mean to you personally?
- Since becoming a believer, how have you transformed from your old self to a new you?
- Reflect on a specific instance where true repentance has brought positive changes in your relationship with God and others. How does that make you feel?

**Bonus Question:** Are there areas in your life where you are finding it difficult to see personal transformation and spiritual growth? What could be the reasons you are finding it challenging?

# NOTES

# Day 19: Burden of the Word

As we progress on our journey of knowing God for ourselves, today, we focus on embracing the burden of the Word. In this context, the burden of the Word is a profound sense of responsibility, urgency, and conviction that weighs heavily on our hearts until we respond to it. The burden of the Word goes beyond just a spiritual revelation or discernment. When God bestows this burden upon us, it is akin to receiving a divine assignment that demands our attention and obedience. It compels us to faithfully steward the message He has entrusted to us.

Embracing the burden of the Word means yielding to God's call, allowing it to deeply influence our hearts and guide our actions. This requires stepping out in faith, and trusting in God's wisdom and timing as we respond to His call. By embracing this burden, we open ourselves to God's transformative work within us, guiding us toward His purposes and shaping our journey of faith. In this way, we not only acknowledge God's sovereignty but also actively participate in His divine plan for humanity.

As we reflect upon the burden of the Word, let's freely open our hearts to receive the burdens God places on us, and faithfully steward His message, sharing it boldly and compassionately wherever and with whomever He leads us.

**Reference Scriptures**

- Jeremiah 20:9
- Ezekiel 3:10-11
- 1 Corinthians 9:16

**Reflection Questions**

- Reflect on moments when you have felt a burden—a divine revelation prompting you to do something. How did you respond, and what impact did it have?
- In what ways do you think the burden of the Word contributes to your role as a minister of the Word and an ambassador of Christ?
- How can you discern between a burden from God and a personal desire or ambition? What are the factors that distinguish them?

# NOTES

# Day 20: Prayerful Reflection

As we continue on this journey of knowing God for ourselves, let's set aside dedicated time to engage in reflective prayer, seeking a clearer awareness of God's presence in our lives and guidance for the path ahead.

The following steps provide a structured approach reflecting common practices and principles for effective reflection:

- **Reality** – What is your reality right now. Be honest about what is going on within you and around you even if it hurts.

- **Reflection** – Seek a truthful perspective from the Word. Take time to process your experiences in light of your faith and your understanding of God

- **Revelation** – Wait for insight and revelation to emerge. Be attentive to subtle signs, divine nudges, and moments of clarity that unveil deeper truths about yourself, your circumstances, and your relationship with God.

- **Respond** – Be spurred on to new action or continue with a renewed sense of purpose and motivation

Through this intentional reflection, let's open our hearts to the whispers of the Holy Spirit, allowing His promptings to guide and strengthen our connection with God.

**Reference Scriptures**

- Philippians 4:6-7
- 1 Thessalonians 5:16-19
- James 5:16

**Reflection Questions**

- What specific methods or practices (e.g., journaling, meditation) do you currently use to enhance your reflective practice? What impact has this had on your spiritual growth?

- What aspects of your relationship with God do you feel need further exploration or understanding?

- How can prayer enhance the depth of your relationship with God?

# NOTES

# Day 21: Pursuing Spiritual Growth

Building upon the practice of prayerful reflection, today, let's focus on actively pursuing our spiritual growth — a commitment to ongoing learning, self-reflection, and transformation both individually and within the community of believers. Spiritual growth encompasses various facets, including expanding our knowledge and deepening our understanding of Scripture, nurturing spiritual disciplines, cultivating intimacy with God, and actively living out our faith. Engaging in meaningful fellowship, accountability, and discipleship within a supportive community can significantly contribute to our spiritual growth and development.

Let's consider practical strategies and intentional steps we can take to continue to grow in our faith.

**Reference Scriptures**

- 2 Peter 3:18
- Colossians 2:6-7
- Ephesians 4:15-16

**Reflection Questions**

- How do you define spiritual growth, and what role does it play in your pursuit of knowing God for yourself?
- In what ways do you actively engage in personal discipleship, seeking to increase your understanding of God and His Word?
- Reflect on the significance of community in your spiritual growth. How do you contribute to and benefit from the community of believers in your life?

**Bonus Question:** Are there specific areas of your spiritual life where you feel the need for growth or transformation? What steps can you take to address those areas?

# NOTES

# Day 22: Carrying Your Cross Daily (Part 1)

Today, let's explore Jesus' call for those who want to be his disciples to deny themselves and carry their cross daily. Jesus was having a reality talk that following him is not easy. Denying self is an absolute surrender to God and is an essential element for our growth and intimacy with him. The concept of carrying our cross daily extends beyond mere physical burdens; it includes the spiritual and emotional challenges we encounter in our walk with God.

Jesus's words serve as a reminder that following him is marked by sacrifice, perseverance, and dedication to his ministry, even in the face of challenges and adversity. It calls us to embrace a lifestyle of self-denial, where we surrender our ambitions, preferences, and selfish desires to God's Will. This act of surrender is not a one-off event but rather an ongoing process of self-denial and embracing the life Christ offers. As we ponder this reality, let's consider its significance in shaping our spiritual journey and advancing the Kingdom of God.

**Reference Scriptures**

- Luke 9:23
- Galatians 5:24
- 2 Corinthians 4:10

**Reflection Questions**

- How do you interpret the idea of 'carrying your cross daily' as a requirement for being a disciple of Jesus?
- What does it mean to deny yourself as a follower of Christ?
- Reflect on instances in the Bible where individuals demonstrated self-denial and a willingness to bear their cross for the sake of the Gospel. What lessons can you draw from those examples?

**Bonus Question:** In what ways do you see the concept of self-denial and taking up the cross reflected in Jesus' own life and teachings?

# NOTES

# Day 23: Carrying Your Cross Daily (Part 2)

Yesterday, we explored the broader concept of self-denial and carrying our cross daily. Today, let's turn our focus inward and reflect on our personal experiences of self-denial and carrying the cross on our spiritual journey.

Denying ourselves and carrying our cross daily involves identifying and addressing areas of our lives where personal desires, comforts, and responses to life come into conflict with the Word. It requires a willingness to confront and address these areas, aligning our thoughts, actions, and attitudes with biblical principles.

As we reflect on our individual experiences, let's consider how we can embrace self-denial and carry our cross daily in tangible ways, allowing these practices to shape and strengthen our walk with God.

**Reference Scriptures**

- Galatians 2:20
- Romans 12:1
- Philippians 3:10

**Reflection Questions**

- Reflecting on your spiritual journey, highlight instances where you have demonstrated self-denial for the sake of your faith. What impact did this have on your spiritual growth and relationship with God?

- How easy or challenging do you find the concept of self-denial in your daily life? Are there areas where you struggle to put God first?

- Mark 8:35 talks about whoever desires to save his soul will lose it, but whoever loses his soul for Jesus' and the gospel's sake will save it. What personal meaning or significance do you draw from this Scripture?

**Bonus Question:** How can you actively cultivate a heart that cherishes Jesus, ensuring that your acts of self-denial and carrying your cross are motivated by genuine love and devotion to things of God?

# NOTES

# Day 24: Embracing God's Grace

Over the past two days, we explored the cost of being a follower of Christ, realising that it requires self-sacrifice, stepping outside our comfort zones, and embracing challenges as opportunities to nurture our relationship with God. We find in Scripture that we cannot consistently please God through our own strength; we need the help of the Holy Spirit and God's grace.

Grace is a central concept in Christianity, representing God's unmerited favour and kindness toward us. It is through grace that Christians believe they are saved, redeemed, and empowered to live a life aligned with God's Will. As we continue our journey of knowing God for ourselves, let's explore the extravagance of God's grace, understand its radical power, and reflect on how we can tap into this incredible gift to make our Christian walk a more joyful experience in all seasons of our lives.

**Reference Scriptures**

- Ephesians 2:8-9
- Romans 3:23-24
- Titus 2:11-12

**Reflection Questions**

- How do you define God's grace in your own words? What are some signs or experiences that indicate God's grace is actively working in your life?
- How can understanding and accepting God's grace influence how you approach challenges and setbacks in your Christian walk?
- How does the awareness of God's grace inspire gratitude and humility in your walk with Him?

**Bonus Question:** In what practical ways can you extend God's grace to others in your community and beyond?

# NOTES

# Day 25. Discovering Your Purpose

As we continue in our walk with God and deepen our relationship with him, understanding and living out his purpose for our lives is important and worth it. In its simplest form, purpose is defined as the reason why something exists or was created to do. Just as a compass guides a traveller on their journey, understanding our purpose provides direction and meaning for our lives. It makes navigating the complexities of life much easier.

There is a plethora of information out there about purpose, how to find it, how to live it, and how to sustain it. Today, let's engage with some of the questions that can help us to discern and confirm our unique purpose here on earth.

**Reference Scriptures**

- Proverbs 20:5
- Jeremiah 29:11
- Romans 12:2

**Reflection Questions**

- What makes you happy and deeply satisfies you?
- What areas do you demonstrate natural talent and proficiency?
- What would you attempt to do if you knew you could not fail?
- When you look out at the world, what breaks your heart the most?
- What altruistic pursuits would you dedicate yourself to if financial limitations were not a factor?

Answering these questions honestly allows your desires and abilities to shine through and a few things that look something like your purpose to emerge. As an illustration, if you find that your purpose is teaching, it is useful to know who and what you are meant to teach. Once you figure this out, you can be more intentional in investing time and effort into gaining the necessary knowledge, skills, and connections needed to be successful in your teaching vocation. When we have a clear vision of what needs to be done and why, it does help in overcoming barriers and discouragements that threaten the course of what we believe God has called us to do.

# NOTES

# Day 26: Functioning in Your Purpose

As our relationship with God grows, we gain clarity and insight into His plans for our lives. The Bible teaches us that we are God's handiwork, created with specific purposes that He has predetermined for us. For some, this can be a groundbreaking music ministry, and for others, it may not be limited to one specific area and may evolve based on our stage of life, spiritual maturity, and the needs of those around us. As we continue our journey of knowing God for ourselves, let's now shift our focus to understanding and embracing his unique purpose or calling in our lives.

**Reference Scriptures**

- Ephesians 2:10
- 1 Corinthians 12:4-6
- Romans 12:6-8

**Reflection Questions**

- What do you understand by the term purpose? How do you see it intersecting with your personal fulfillment and God's Will for humanity?

- Reflecting on your current endeavours, how aligned do you feel they are with God's purpose for your life? Are there areas where you feel called to make adjustments or realignments?

- How open and willing are you to be led by God and adapt to new opportunities or roles that may help advance His purpose for your life?

# NOTES

# Day 27: Finding Beauty in Discouragement

In our faith journey and pursuit of our life's purpose, we inevitably encounter moments of discouragement. Discouragement can be defined as a feeling of loss of confidence or enthusiasm, often resulting from setbacks, challenges, or unmet expectations. It manifests in various ways, such as feelings of inadequacy, self-doubt, or disillusionment, and has the potential to hinder our progress.

Amid the trials and tribulations, there is an opportunity to find beauty – to learn, to grow, and to emerge stronger than before. We are presented with a chance to reflect on our experiences, reassess our goals, and deepen our understanding of ourselves and our faith. These moments of adversity serve as catalysts for personal growth and character development — we discover inner reservoirs of strength and resilience that we may not have known existed within us.

In moments of discouragement, exercising discernment and wisdom is crucial to determine whether to persist and persevere or acknowledge that continuing in a certain direction may lead us away from our purpose and become distracting. Sometimes, God signals a need for course correction, prompting us to re-evaluate our direction and re-align with His Will. Through prayerful reflections and seeking counsel from trusted people around us, we can discern the source and significance of the discouragement. Seeking guidance and support provides valuable insights and perspectives, helping us to confidently navigate through discouraging seasons with clarity and conviction.

Using the Scriptures and reflection questions provided, let's explore how we can rise above discouragement and continue on our journey with resilience and determination.

**Reference Scriptures**

- James 1:2-4
- 2 Corinthians 4:16-18
- 2 Corinthians 12:9-10

**Reflection Questions**

- How do you personally define discouragement, and what are some common triggers or sources of discouragement in your life?
- Reflect on a time when you felt discouraged in pursuit of your faith and life's purpose. What were the circumstances, and how did it impact your motivation and progress?
- What effective strategies or coping mechanisms have you utilised or can you utilise to overcome discouragement and stay focused on your purpose?

# NOTES

# Day 28: Knowing and Overcoming the Enemy

As we navigate our faith journey, it is important to recognise that we also have an adversary – the devil – who actively works against us. The Bible describes him as a cunning enemy whose aim is to steal, kill, and destroy. One of his primary tactics is to instill fear in us, preventing us from stepping out and fully embracing who we are in Christ and his purpose for us.

It is, therefore, essential to equip and empower ourselves to overcome the enemy's schemes. By cultivating discernment and spiritual wisdom, we can thwart his schemes and stay aligned with God's purpose for our lives. As we remain vigilant and steadfast in our faith, we fortify our relationship with God, laying a solid and unshakeable foundation to sustain a fruitful spiritual journey anchored in His grace and truth.

**Reference Scriptures**

- Ephesians 6:12
- 1 Peter 5:8-9
- James 4:7

**Reflection Questions**

- How do you recognise the enemy's attacks on your life? What are some common tactics or strategies he uses to frustrate your spiritual growth and purpose?
- Reflect on a time when you felt under attack by the enemy. How did you respond, and what did you learn from that experience?
- What biblical principles or strategies have you found effective in combating the enemy's assaults on your life? How do you stay rooted in God's truth and be who he has called you to be?

# NOTES

# Day 29: Strength in Godly Friendships

God designed us to walk alongside one another, support, and uplift each other in our faith journeys. Godly friendships are a necessity in our spiritual life and growth. They serve as anchors that keep us rooted in our faith, offering strength and support both in good and not-so-good times.

Through our friendships, whether in our small groups, accountability partners, or spiritual mentors and coaches, we discover the power of vulnerability, transparency, and mutual support in helping us stay grounded in our faith and grow in our understanding and experience of God's love and grace. We do not only find encouragement but also challenge one another to grow in love and good deeds, fostering a community where everyone is uplifted and strengthened.

As we reflect on the quality of our relationships within our faith community, let's consider how we can contribute to fostering a culture of support, encouragement, and accountability among believers. By nurturing these bonds, we build a community where everyone is valued, supported, and empowered to thrive in their walk with God.

### Reference Scriptures

- Ecclesiastes 4:9-10
- Hebrews 10:24-25
- Proverbs 27:17

### Reflection Questions

- On a scale of 0 to 10, (0 being disconnected and 10 being very close-knit and supportive), what is your relationship like within your church community?
- Reflect on a time when a godly friendship or accountability partner supported you through a challenging season. How did their presence and encouragement strengthen you?
- What specific actions can you take to contribute to creating a culture of support, encouragement, and accountability among believers?

# NOTES

# Day 30: Serving the Lord with Heart, Body and Soul

As we near the culmination of our journey in knowing God for ourselves, it is crucial to reflect on how we serve the Lord with our entire being – heart, body, and soul. At the end of our days, when we stand before the Lord, we aspire to hear the words, "…Well done, good and faithful servant!" (Matthew 25:21). These words encourage us to dedicate ourselves wholeheartedly to His service, striving to honour Him in all that we do.

Additionally, we are reminded of the importance of authenticity and sincerity in our devotion. Jesus cautioned against mere lip service, saying, "…I never knew you. Away from me, you evildoers!" (Matthew 7:23). This sobering reminder urges us to go beyond surface-level commitment and instead cultivate a deep, genuine relationship with God. It calls us to allow His refining fire to burn away any impurities within us, leaving behind a fervent dedication to His Will and purpose.

Let's explore what it truly means to serve the Lord with sincerity and devotion, aligning our actions with His Will and purpose for our lives. As we do so, may we find fulfillment and joy in serving him with all our hearts, body, and soul.

**Reference Scriptures**

- Colossians 3:23-24
- 1 Corinthians 15:58
- Romans 12:1-2

**Reflection Questions**

- How are you currently serving the Lord? Are there areas where you feel called to commit and devote?
- Reflect on the Parable of the Bags of Gold found in Matthew 25:14-30. In what ways are you stewarding what God has given you?
- What areas of your life do you sense God is refining, purifying, or challenging you to surrender to His will?

**Bonus Question:** How can you ensure that your service to the Lord is not merely outward actions but stems from genuine love and devotion to advance His Kingdom?

# NOTES

# Day 31: Thriving in Your Faith Sustainably

As we conclude our 31-day journey of knowing God for ourselves, it is worth noting the importance of living our faith sustainably. Sustaining our faith requires consistency, perseverance, and a deep-rooted connection with God. This entails tirelessly nurturing our spiritual lives to maintain a strong and enduring relationship with God, moving beyond short-term enthusiasm to a lasting bond with Him.

To thrive in our faith sustainably requires embedding practices and habits that support our spiritual growth into our daily lives. Regular prayer, consistent study of God's Word, active participation in fellowship with other believers, and engaging in acts of service and worship are all essential components of this process. These practices not only nourish our relationship with God but also provide a stable foundation upon which we can build our faith. By prioritising these habits, we ensure that our spiritual journey is not just a temporary phase but a lifelong commitment characterised by growth, resilience, and depth.

As we reflect on our journey so far, let's consider how we can continue to thrive in our faith sustainably. Let's envision a future where our relationship with God continues to deepen, where our faith is marked by steadfastness and growth, and where we remain anchored in His love and grace. Let's be filled with confidence to echo the same sentiments of apostle Paul, "I have fought the good fight, I have finished the race, I have kept the faith" (2 Timothy 4:7).

**Reference Scriptures**

- Jeremiah 17:7-8
- Isaiah 40:31
- Hebrews 12:1-2

**Reflection Questions**

- How have you personally experienced growth in your relationship with God during this devotional experience? Reflect on specific moments or practices that have contributed to this growth.

- Drawing from the parable of the wise and foolish builders found in Matthew 7:24-27, how can you anchor yourself more firmly in your relationship with God? Consider practical steps you can take to strengthen this foundation in your daily life.

- What potential challenges or distractions do you anticipate encountering on your journey of serving the Lord? How can you proactively address these challenges and stay committed to your faith?

**Bonus Question:** Imagine yourself five years from now. How do you envision your relationship with God and your faith journey at that point? Consider setting specific spiritual goals or milestones to guide your growth over this period.

Congratulations on completing this devotional experience with me! Over the past 31 days, we've engaged in introspective reflections, grappled with challenging questions, and embarked on a journey of personal growth and spiritual renewal.

By investing time and effort into nurturing our relationship with God, we have laid a solid foundation for continued spiritual flourishing. Through exploring topics such as faith, obedience, intimacy with God, and purpose, we've gained valuable insights into the depths of God's love and the abundance of His grace.

As you reflect on your journey through this devotional, remember that spiritual growth is not a destination but a lifelong pursuit. May the insights gained and lessons learned during these 31 days fuel your ongoing adventure with God, inspiring you to seek Him more earnestly, trust Him more deeply, and serve Him more wholeheartedly.

Moving forward, I pray that you:

- continue to prioritise your relationship with God, intentionally carving out time for prayer, meditation, and study of His Word
- continue to cultivate a heart of gratitude, recognising God's faithfulness in every season of your life, and
- remain open to the leading of the Holy Spirit as He guides you into greater depths of intimacy and purpose.

May the truths you've encountered in this devotional take root in your Spirit, empowering you to radiate God's love in the world. Keep pressing forward in faith embracing the abundant life that God has prepared for you.

Much Love

Ester

# NOTES

## Reference Scriptures

I hope these verses enhance your devotional experience!

| Day | Scriptures |
|---|---|
| **Day 1: The Trinity** | Matthew 28:19 - Therefore go and make disciples of all nations, baptising them in the name of the Father and of the Son and of the Holy Spirit.<br><br>2 Corinthians 13:14 - May the grace of the Lord Jesus Christ, and the love of God, and the fellowship of the Holy Spirit be with you all.<br><br>John 14:26 - But the Advocate, the Holy Spirit, whom the Father will send in my name, will teach you all things and will remind you of everything I have said to you. |
| **Day 2: God's Character** | Exodus 34:6-7 - …The Lord, the Lord, the compassionate and gracious God, slow to anger, abounding in love and faithfulness, maintaining love to thousands, and forgiving wickedness, rebellion and sin…<br><br>Lamentations 3:22-23 - Because of the Lord's great love, we are not consumed, for his compassions never fail. They are new every morning; great is your faithfulness.<br><br>Romans 8:28 - And we know that in all things God works for the good of those who love him, who have been called according to his purpose. |
| **Day 3: God's Attributes** | Psalm 139:7-10 - Where can I go from your Spirit? Where can I flee from your presence? If I go up to the heavens, you are there; if I make my bed in the depths, you are there. If I rise on the wings of the dawn, if I settle on the far side of the sea, even there your hand will guide me, your right hand will hold me fast.<br><br>Isaiah 40:28 - Do you not know? Have you not heard? The Lord is the everlasting God, the Creator of the ends of the earth. He will not grow tired or weary, and his understanding no one can fathom.<br><br>Hebrews 4:13 - Nothing in all creation is hidden from God's sight. Everything is uncovered and laid bare before the eyes of him to whom we must give account. |

| | |
|---|---|
| **Day 4: God's Names** | Exodus 3:14 - God said to Moses, 'I am who I am. This is what you are to say to the Israelites: 'I am has sent me to you.' |
| | Isaiah 9:6 - For to us a child is born, to us a son is given, and the government will be on his shoulders. And he will be called Wonderful Counsellor, Mighty God, Everlasting Father, Prince of Peace. |
| | Philippians 2:9-11 - Therefore God exalted him to the highest place and gave him the name that is above every name, that at the name of Jesus, every knee should bow, in heaven and on earth and under the earth, and every tongue acknowledge that Jesus Christ is Lord, to the glory of God the Father. |
| **Day 5: Faith and Trust** | Hebrews 11:1 - Now faith is confidence in what we hope for and assurance about what we do not see. |
| | Proverbs 3:5-6 - Trust in the Lord with all your heart and lean not on your own understanding; in all your ways submit to him, and he will make your paths straight. |
| | Mark 11:22-24 - Have faith in God,' Jesus answered. 'Truly I tell you, if anyone says to this mountain, 'Go, throw yourself into the sea,' and does not doubt in their heart but believes that what they say will happen, it will be done for them. Therefore, I tell you, whatever you ask for in prayer, believe that you have received it, and it will be yours. |
| **Day 6: Intimacy with God** | Jeremiah 29:13 - You will seek me and find me when you seek me with all your heart. |
| | Psalm 27:8 - My heart says of you, 'Seek his face!' Your face, Lord, I will seek. |
| | John 15:5 - I am the vine; you are the branches. If you remain in me and I in you, you will bear much fruit; apart from me, you can do nothing. |

| | |
|---|---|
| **Day 7: Identity In Christ** | 2 Corinthians 5:17 - Therefore, if anyone is in Christ, the new creation has come: The old has gone, the new is here!<br><br>1 Peter 2:9 - But you are a chosen people, a royal priesthood, a holy nation, God's special possession, that you may declare the praises of him who called you out of darkness into his wonderful light.<br><br>Romans 8:17 - Now if we are children, then we are heirs—heirs of God and co-heirs with Christ, if indeed we share in his sufferings in order that we may also share in his glory. |
| **Day 8: Nurturing Spiritual Disciplines** | 1 Timothy 4:7-8 - Have nothing to do with godless myths and old wives' tales; rather, train yourself to be godly. For physical training is of some value, but godliness has value for all things, holding promise for both the present life and the life to come.<br><br>Psalm 119:11 - I have hidden your word in my heart that I might not sin against you.<br><br>Colossians 3:16 - Let the message of Christ dwell among you richly as you teach and admonish one another with all wisdom through psalms, hymns, and songs from the Spirit, singing to God with gratitude in your hearts. |
| **Day 9: Discerning God's Voice** | John 10:27 - My sheep listen to my voice; I know them, and they follow me.<br><br>1 Kings 19:11-12 - The Lord said, 'Go out and stand on the mountain in the presence of the Lord, for the Lord is about to pass by.' Then a great and powerful wind tore the mountains apart and shattered the rocks before the Lord, but the Lord was not in the wind. After the wind there was an earthquake, but the Lord was not in the earthquake. After the earthquake came a fire, but the Lord was not in the fire. And after the fire came to a gentle whisper.<br><br>Isaiah 30:21 - Whether you turn to the right or to the left, your ears will hear a voice behind you, saying, 'This is the way; walk in it.' |

| | |
|---|---|
| **Day 10: The Holy Spirit** | Acts 1:8 - But you will receive power when the Holy Spirit comes on you; and you will be my witnesses in Jerusalem, and in all Judea and Samaria, and to the ends of the earth.<br><br>John 14:26 - But the Advocate, the Holy Spirit, whom the Father will send in my name, will teach you all things and will remind you of everything I have said to you.<br><br>Romans 8:26 - In the same way, the Spirit helps us in our weakness. We do not know what we ought to pray for, but the Spirit himself intercedes for us through wordless groans. |
| **Day 11: Obedience** | 1 John 2:3-6 - We know that we have come to know him if we keep his commands. Whoever says, 'I know him,' but does not do what he commands is a liar, and the truth is not in that person. But if anyone obeys his word, love for God is truly made complete in them. This is how we know we are in him: Whoever claims to live in him must live as Jesus did.<br><br>James 1:22 - Do not merely listen to the word, and so deceive yourselves. what it says whether you are slaves to sin, which leads to death, or to obedience, which leads to righteousness?<br><br>Romans 6:16 - Don't you know that when you offer yourselves to someone as obedient slaves, you are slaves of the one you obey |
| **Day 12: Audacious Faith** | Matthew 17:20 - He replied, 'Because you have so little faith. Truly, I tell you, if you have faith as small as a mustard seed, you can say to this mountain, 'Move from here to there,' and it will move. Nothing will be impossible for you.'<br><br>Hebrews 11:1 - Now faith is confidence in what we hope for and assurance about what we do not see.<br><br>Mark 9:23 - … 'Everything is possible for one who believes.' |

| Day 13: Cultivating Audacious Faith | Romans 10:17 - Consequently, faith comes from hearing the message, and the message is heard through the word about Christ. |
| --- | --- |
| | Hebrews 11:6 - And without faith, it is impossible to please God, because anyone who comes to him must believe that he exists and that he rewards those who earnestly seek him. |
| | James 1:6 - But when you ask, you must believe and not doubt, because the one who doubts is like a wave of the sea, blown and tossed by the wind. |
| Day 14: The Power of Our Words | Proverbs 18:21 - The tongue has the power of life and death, and those who love it will eat its fruit. |
| | Ephesians 4:29 - Do not let any unwholesome talk come out of your mouths, but only what is helpful for building others up according to their needs, that it may benefit those who listen. |
| | Matthew 12:36 - But I tell you that everyone will have to give account on the day of judgment for every empty word they have spoken. |
| Day 15: Ambassadors of Christ | 2 Corinthians 5:20 - We are therefore Christ's ambassadors, as though God were making his appeal through us. We implore you on Christ's behalf: Be reconciled to God. |
| | Ephesians 6:19-20 - Pray also for me, that whenever I speak, words may be given me so that I will fearlessly make known the mystery of the gospel, for which I am an ambassador in chains. Pray that I may declare it fearlessly, as I should. |
| | Philippians 2:13 - for it is God who works in you to will and to act in order to fulfil his good purpose. |

| Day 16: The Call to Evangelism | Matthew 28:19-20 - Therefore go and make disciples of all nations, baptising them in the name of the Father and of the Son and of the Holy Spirit, and teaching them to obey everything I have commanded you. And surely, I am with you always, to the very end of the age. |
|---|---|
| | Acts 1:8 - But you will receive power when the Holy Spirit comes on you, and you will be my witnesses in Jerusalem, and in all Judea and Samaria, and to the ends of the earth. |
| | Romans 10:14 - How, then, can they call on the one they have not believed in? And how can they believe in the one whom they have not heard? And how can they hear without someone preaching to them? |
| Day 17: Overcoming Barriers to Intimacy with God | Psalm 139:23-24 - Search me, God, and know my heart; test me and know my anxious thoughts. See if there is any offensive way in me, and lead me in the way everlasting. |
| | Proverbs 18:24 - One who has unreliable friends soon comes to ruin, but there is a friend who sticks closer than a brother. |
| | Hebrews 4:16 – Let us then approach God's throne of grace with confidence, so that we may receive mercy and find grace to help us in our time of need. |
| Day 18: The Transformative Power of Repentance | Acts 3:19 - Repent, then, and turn to God, so that your sins may be wiped out, that times of refreshing may come from the Lord. |
| | Ezekiel 18:30 - Therefore, you Israelites, I will judge each of you according to your own ways, declares the Sovereign Lord. Repent! Turn away from all your offenses; then sin will not be your downfall. |
| | 1 John 1:9 - If we confess our sins, he is faithful and just and will forgive us our sins and purify us from all unrighteousness. |
| Day 19: Burden of the Word | Jeremiah 20:9 - But if I say, 'I will not mention his word or speak anymore in his name,' his word is in my heart like a fire, a fire shut up in my bones. I am weary of holding it in; indeed, I cannot. |
| | Ezekiel 3:10-11 - And he said to me, 'Son of man, listen carefully and take to heart all the words I speak to you. Go now to your people in exile and speak to them. Say to them, 'This is what the Sovereign Lord says,' whether they listen or fail to listen.' |
| | 1 Corinthians 9:16 - For when I preach the gospel, I cannot boast, since I am compelled to preach. Woe to me if I do not preach the gospel! |

| | |
|---|---|
| **Day 20: Prayerful Reflections** | Philippians 4:6-7 - Do not be anxious about anything, but in every situation, by prayer and petition, with thanksgiving, present your requests to God. And the peace of God, which transcends all understanding, will guard your hearts and your minds in Christ Jesus.<br><br>1 Thessalonians 5:16-19 - Rejoice always, pray continually, give thanks in all circumstances; for this is God's Will for you in Christ Jesus. Do not quench the Spirit<br><br>James 5:16 - Therefore confess your sins to each other and pray for each other so that you may be healed. The prayer of a righteous person is powerful and effective. |
| **Day 21: Pursuing Personal Spiritual Growth** | 2 Peter 3:18 - But grow in the grace and knowledge of our Lord and Savior Jesus Christ. To him be glory both now and forever! Amen.<br><br>Colossians 2:6-7 - So then, just as you received Christ Jesus as Lord, continue to live your lives in him, rooted and built up in him, strengthened in the faith as you were taught, and overflowing with thankfulness.<br><br>Ephesians 4:15-16 - Instead, speaking the truth in love, we will grow to become in every respect the mature body of him who is the head, that is, Christ. From him, the whole body, joined and held together by every supporting ligament, grows and builds itself up in love, as each part does its work. |
| **Day 22: Carrying Your Cross Daily (Part 1)** | Luke 9:23 - Then he said to them all: 'Whoever wants to be my disciple must deny themselves and take up their cross daily and follow me.'<br><br>Galatians 5:24 - Those who belong to Christ Jesus have crucified the flesh with its passions and desires.<br><br>2 Corinthians 4:10 - We always carry around in our body the death of Jesus, so that the life of Jesus may also be revealed in our body. |

| | |
|---|---|
| **Day 23: Carrying Your Cross Daily (Part 2)** | Galatians 2:20 - I have been crucified with Christ, and I no longer live, but Christ lives in me. The life I now live in the body, I live by faith in the Son of God, who loved me and gave himself for me.<br><br>Romans 12:1 - Therefore, I urge you, brothers and sisters, in view of God's mercy, to offer your bodies as a living sacrifice, holy and pleasing to God—this is your true and proper worship.<br><br>Philippians 3:10 - I want to know Christ—yes, to know the power of his resurrection and participation in his sufferings, becoming like him in his death. |
| **Day 24: Embracing God's Grace** | Ephesians 2:8-9 - For it is by grace you have been saved, through faith— and this is not from yourselves, it is the gift of God—not by works, so that no one can boast.<br><br>Romans 3:23-24 - for all have sinned and fall short of the glory of God, and all are justified freely by his grace through the redemption that came by Christ Jesus.<br><br>Titus 2:11-12 - For the grace of God has appeared that offers salvation to all people. It teaches us to say 'No' to ungodliness and worldly passions and to live self-controlled, upright and godly lives in this present age. |
| **Day 25: Discovering Your Purpose** | Proverbs 20:5 - The purposes of a person's heart are deep waters, but one who has insight draws them out.<br><br>Jeremiah 29:11 - 'For I know the plans I have for you,' declares the Lord, 'plans to prosper you and not to harm you, plans to give you hope and a future.'<br><br>Romans 12:2 - Do not conform to the pattern of this world, but be transformed by the renewing of your mind. Then you will be able to test and approve what God's will is—his good, pleasing and perfect will. |

| | |
|---|---|
| **Day 26: Functioning in Your Purpose** | Ephesians 2:10 - For we are God's handiwork, created in Christ Jesus to do good works, which God prepared in advance for us to do.<br><br>1 Corinthians 12:4-6 - There are different kinds of gifts, but the same Spirit distributes them. There are different kinds of service, but the same Lord. There are different kinds of working, but in all of them and in everyone it is the same God at work.<br><br>Romans 12:6-8 - We have different gifts, according to the grace given to each of us. If your gift is prophesying, then prophesy in accordance with your faith; if it is serving, then serve; if it is teaching, then teach; if it is to encourage, then give encouragement; if it is giving, then give generously; if it is to lead, do it diligently; if it is to show mercy, do it cheerfully. |
| **Day 27: Finding Beauty in Discouragement** | James 1:2-4 - Consider it pure joy, my brothers and sisters, whenever you face trials of many kinds because you know that the testing of your faith produces perseverance. Let perseverance finish its work so that you may be mature and complete, not lacking anything.<br><br>2 Corinthians 4:16-18 - Therefore we do not lose heart. Though outwardly we are wasting away, yet inwardly we are being renewed day by day. For our light and momentary troubles are achieving for us an eternal glory that far outweighs them all. So we fix our eyes not on what is seen, but on what is unseen, since what is seen is temporary, but what is unseen is eternal.<br><br>2 Corinthians 12:9-10 - But he said to me, 'My grace is sufficient for you, for my power is made perfect in weakness.' Therefore, I will boast all the more gladly about my weaknesses, so that Christ's power may rest on me. That is why, for Christ's sake, I delight in weaknesses, in insults, in hardships, in persecutions, in difficulties. For when I am weak, then I am strong. |

| | |
|---|---|
| **Day 28: Knowing and Overcoming the Enemy** | Ephesians 6:12 - For our struggle is not against flesh and blood, but against the rulers, against the authorities, against the powers of this dark world and against the spiritual forces of evil in the heavenly realms.<br><br>1 Peter 5:8-9 - Be alert and of sober mind. Your enemy, the devil, prowls around like a roaring lion looking for someone to devour. Resist him, standing firm in the faith, because you know that the family of believers throughout the world is undergoing the same kind of suffering.<br><br>James 4:7 - Submit yourselves, then, to God. Resist the devil, and he will flee from you. |
| **Day 29: Strength in Godly Friendships** | Ecclesiastes 4:9-10 - Two are better than one, because they have a good return for their labour: If either of them falls down, one can help the other up.<br><br>Hebrews 10:24-25 - And let us consider how we may spur one another on toward love and good deeds, not giving up meeting together, as some are in the habit of doing, but encouraging one another—and all the more as you see the Day approaching.<br><br>Proverbs 27:17 - As iron sharpens iron, so one person sharpens another. |
| **Day 30: Serving the Lord with Heart, Body, and Soul** | Colossians 3:23-24 - Whatever you do, work at it with all your heart, as working for the Lord, not for human masters, since you know that you will receive an inheritance from the Lord as a reward. It is the Lord Christ you are serving.<br><br>1 Corinthians 15:58 - Therefore, my dear brothers and sisters, stand firm. Let nothing move you. Always give yourselves fully to the work of the Lord, because you know that your labour in the Lord is not in vain.<br><br>Romans 12:1-2 - Therefore, I urge you, brothers and sisters, in view of God's mercy, to offer your bodies as a living sacrifice, holy and pleasing to God—this is your true and proper worship. |

| Day 31: Thriving in Your Faith Sustainably | Jeremiah 17:7-8 - But blessed is the one who trusts in the Lord, whose confidence is in him. They will be like a tree planted by the water that sends out its roots by the stream. It does not fear when heat comes; its leaves are always green. It has no worries in a year of drought and never fails to bear fruit.

Isaiah 40:31 - But those who hope in the Lord will renew their strength. They will soar on wings like eagles; they will run and not grow weary; they will walk and not be faint.

Hebrews 12:1-2 - Therefore, since we are surrounded by such a great cloud of witnesses, let us throw off everything that hinders and the sin that so easily entangles. And let us run with perseverance the race marked out for us, fixing our eyes on Jesus, the pioneer and perfecter of faith. |
|---|---|

www.ingramcontent.com/pod-product-compliance
Lightning Source LLC
Chambersburg PA
CBHW081625100526
44590CB00021B/3604